ICON
Grammar Supplement

Donald Freeman

Kathleen Graves

Linda Lee

Lisa Varandani

**McGraw-Hill
ESL/ELT**

3

icon!
Grammar Supplement

Donald Freeman

Kathleen Graves

Linda Lee

Lisa Varandani

McGraw-Hill
ESL/ELT

ICON 3 Grammar Supplement

Published by McGraw-Hill ESL/ELT, a business unit of The McGraw-Hill Companies, Inc. 1221 Avenue of the Americas, New York, NY 10020. Copyright © 2007 by The McGraw-Hill Companies, Inc. All rights reserved. No part of this publication may be reproduced or distributed in any form or by any means, or stored in a database or retrieval system, without the prior written consent of The McGraw-Hill Companies, Inc., including, but not limited to, in any network or other electronic storage or transmission, or broadcast for distance learning.

ISBN 13: 978-0-07-329865-8
ISBN 10: 0-07-329865-4

1 2 3 4 5 6 7 8 9 10   D 22 20 02   12 11 10 09 08 07

Editorial director: Tina B. Carver
Senior managing Editor: Arley Gray
Production manager: Juanita Thompson
Production coordinator: James D. Gwyn
Interior designer: Nesbitt Graphics, Inc.
Cover designer: Nesbitt Graphics, Inc.

ICON 3 Components

Student Book	0-07-255049-X
Workbook	0-07-255050-3
Teacher's Manual	0-07-255051-1
Audio Cassettes	0-07-225052-X
Audio CDs	0-07-255053-8
EZ-Tests	0-07-335291-8
Assessment Package	0-07-353384-X

www.esl-elt.mcgraw-hill.com

Impreso en Colombia   Printed in Colombia
Impreso por Litocamargo Ltda.

The McGraw·Hill Companies

Contents

1-1 COMPARATIVES WITH NOUNS

❶ You can use the structure **more of** + noun in comparative sentences.

> Darrell is **more of a friend** than a father.
> Carol is **more of an executive** than a manager.

❷ Use **more of** + compound noun to give more information about the nouns in comparative sentences.

> I'm more of a **city** person than an **outdoors** person.
> Bill is more of a **tennis** person than a **golf** person.

A. Unscramble the sentences. In some cases there are two correct answers.

1. a friend holiday / is / Thanksgiving / of / more / a family holiday / than /.

   _____

2. than / Joe's Sandwich Shop / a casual place / a dressy place / more / is / of /.

   _____

3. a tea drinker / Lisa / a coffee drinker / is / more / of / than /.

   _____

4. Greg / of / is / a people person / more / than / a computer person /.

   _____

5. a cake person / more / is / of / than / Bill / a potato chip person /.

   _____

B. Finish the sentences about the people you know. Use comparative forms.

1. _____ is more of an outdoors person than a city person.

2. _____ is more of a jeans and t-shirts guy than a suit guy.

3. _____ is more of a salad person than a hamburger person.

4. I'm more of _____ than _____.

5. My friend _____ is more of _____ than _____.

6. _____ is more of _____.

1-2 TAG QUESTIONS WITH MODALS

❶ You can use tag questions in sentences with modals. Use the same modal in the tag and the statement.

> She **can't** come, **can she?**
> She **will** come, **won't she?**
> I **should** call, **shouldn't I?**

❷ An affirmative statement takes a negative tag. A negative statement takes an affirmative tag.

> Greg *can* cook dinner, **can't** he?
> He *could* hear us, **couldn't** he?
> You **won't** go, *will* you?
> Judy **shouldn't** drive, *should* she?

C. Write the correct modal or the correct tag question to complete each sentence.

1. She shouldn't be scared to interview, _____?

2. He won't call me back, _____?

3. You couldn't, _____?

4. You _____ network for me, won't you?

5. Jenny _____ get a new job, shouldn't she?

6. Dave should schmooze more at work, _____?

7. You can't fix my computer, _____?

8. Aya _____ be the CEO, couldn't she?

9. They _____ get to the office before us, will they?

10. He should send in his resume, _____?

11. You _____ give me a raise, can't you?

12. I _____ look professional, will I?

❶ You can add the suffix *-able* to many regular verbs in order to change the part of speech to an adjective.

Base Verb	Adjective
pass	pass**able**
market	market**able**
live	liv**able**

❷ You can add the suffix *-er* to many regular verbs in order to change the part of speech to a noun. A noun than ends in *-er* is the person or thing that does the action.

Base Verb	Noun
schmooze	schmooz**er**
market	market**er**
work	work**er**
compute	comput**er**

D. Finish the chart with the correct form of the words.

Base Verb	Noun	Adjective
sing		singable
	thinker	
drive		drivable
	fixer	
build		

E. Write the verb, noun, or adjective form of the word in parentheses.

1. I'm not a _____. I like to keep quiet. *(talk)*

2. Andrea is very _____. She's also smart and upbeat. *(like)*

3. My sister got a job as a _____ when she finished cooking school. *(bake)*

4. I believe that anybody is _____ if they want to learn. *(teach)*

5. My computer isn't working very well, but I think it's _____. *(fix)*

6. We can't _____ any more. We're too tired. *(work)*

7. You should _____ the CEO if the company treated you unfairly. *(call)*

8. She doesn't have experience, so she's not very _____. *(hire)*

1-4 DIRECT QUOTATIONS IN WRITING

1 When using direct quotations in writing, use double quotation marks around the quote.

> Ford says, **"**Being a good schmoozer makes you much more marketable.**"**

2 Use a comma to separate the speaker from the quotation. Commas and periods are always inside the quotation.

> "How you appear in social situations is extremely important**,**" adds Ford.

3 Question marks and exclamation points go inside the quotation marks when they are part of the quotation, and outside when they are not.

> Anthony asked, "How can I be more successful**?**"
> Who said "Schmoozing is important"**?**

F. Add the punctuation to each of the sentences. Quotations are underlined.

1. Mr. Thomas says <u>You should always dress up for an interview</u>

2. <u>I'm looking for a new job</u> said Teresa

3. Derek said <u>I'm not a schmoozer</u>

4. Mary asked <u>What's the name of the company</u>

5. <u>Who believes in our company</u> asked the CEO

6. Judy added <u>People who work hard are successful</u>

7. My father always says <u>A good education is all you need to succeed</u>

8. Did she just say <u>I quit</u>

G. Rewrite the dialog below using direct quotations.

Scott Sanders:	In my opinion, if you want to be a CEO you have to get an MBA.
Allison Vann:	I disagree. I always say it's not what you know, but who you know.
Scott Sanders:	That might be true, but a good education is still important.
Allison Vann:	Are you sure you don't work for a university, Mr. Sanders?

1. _____

2. _____

3. _____

4. _____

2-1 FUTURE CONDITIONAL WITH *SHOULD, MAY, MIGHT,* AND *COULD*

❶ You can use modals other than *will* in future conditional sentences.

> If it's sunny, we **might** go for a hike.
> If it's sunny, we **should** go for a hike.
> If it's sunny, we **may** go for a hike

❷ The modals *should, may,* and *might* express less certainty than *will* and *be going to.*

> If you study, you **will** pass the test. *(very certain)*
> If you study, you **should** pass the test. *(probable)*
> If you study, you **may** pass the test. *(possible)*
> If you study, you **might** pass the test. *(possible)*

❸ *Should* is also used for giving advice. *Could* is used to express ability to do something.

> If it's cold outside, you **should** wear a hat. *(advice)*
> If you don't wear a hat, you **could** get sick. *(ability)*

A. Write the modal or negative modal that's true for you.

1. If it's drizzling tomorrow, I _____ take an umbrella.

2. If it's overcast tomorrow, I _____ wear a coat.

3. I _____ be happy if we have a sunny day tomorrow.

4. If we have a cold winter this year, I _____ be surprised.

5. If it's raining cats and dogs Saturday night, I _____ leave my house.

B. Finish the sentences using the future conditional.

1. If it rains this weekend, I might _____.

2. If it snows next summer, I will _____.

3. If Bangkok has frigid weather this year, _____.

4. _____, I may not go to the party.

5. _____, the beach should be very crowded.

6. If it's foggy tomorrow morning, _____.

7. _____, I might not play soccer.

8. We may go skiing _____.

2-2 ARTICLES WITH GEOGRAPHIC NAMES

1 Most singular geographic names do not need an article before them because they are proper nouns. This is true for continents, countries, cities, mountains, lakes, islands, streets, and squares.

> I live in *Arica, Chile.*
> I'm from *Spain,* but I live in *Ireland.*
> *Tokyo* is an exciting city.
> *Lake Powell* is in *Utah.*

2 Use *the* before geographic names that are plural or collective.

> *The* *Galapagos Islands* are part of Ecuador.
> *The* *U.S.A.* is a large country.
> *The* *Himalaya Mountains* are in Asia.

3 Use *the* before the following irregular singular geographic names: rivers, deserts, regions, peninsulas, oceans, and seas.

> *The* *Tiber River* is in Rome.
> *The* *Sahara Desert* is the largest in the world.
> Is *the* *Pacific Ocean* larger than the Atlantic?

C. Write the correct article in the blanks: *the, a, an,* or Ø (no article).

1. _____ Charles River is in _____ Boston.

2. _____ Sahara Desert is the largest desert in the world.

3. The water in _____ Caribbean Sea is clear and blue.

4. I would like to visit _____ Moscow in the winter to see the northern lights.

5. _____ Andes Mountains are in several South American countries.

6. Do you know how high _____ Mount Everest is?

7. We just got back from vacation. We went to _____ France and _____ U.K.

8. _____ Lake Atitlan is in _____ Guatemala.

9. Alaska is the biggest state in _____ United States.

10. _____ Cape Verde Islands are off the coast of _____ Africa.

11. _____ Caracas is the capital of _____ Venezuela.

12. _____ Mount Fuji is a famous symbol of _____ Japan.

❶ When making generalizations, use *a / an* before a singular count noun.

> ***An* island** is surrounded by water.
> ***A* desert** doesn't get a lot of rain.

❷ We use *no article* before a non-count noun or a plural count noun when making general statements.

> **Beaches** in Brazil are wonderful.
> **Ocean water** is salty.
> **Sunshine** is good for you.

❸ We sometimes use *the* before singular count nouns in general statements. Typically this is used with types of animals, musical instruments, technology, and inventions.

> ***The* monkey** is an interesting animal.
> ***The* iPod** has become very popular since it came out.
> I would like to learn to play ***the* violin**.

D. Circle the correct articles for each sentence. Ø = *no article*.

1. Even though we don't always like it, (Ø / the) rain is good for the environment.

2. (Ø / The) tarantula is a large spider that lives in the desert.

3. (A / Ø) peninsula has water on 3 sides of it, but is still connected to land.

4. She isn't very good at (a / the) piano. She should practice more!

5. (Ø / A) mountains are great places to go hiking with your family.

6. (The / A) cell phone is an important part of daily life around the world.

7. (The / Ø) guinea pig is a small, furry animal that is related to (the / a) rabbit.

8. (An / The) electric guitar is an important instrument in rock and roll music.

9. (The / Ø) trees and (a / Ø) grass make a yard look nicer.

10. (Ø / The) clouds can sometimes be depressing.

11. (Ø / A) temperature and (the / Ø) precipitation help determine the climate.

12. (An / Ø) umbrella won't keep you very dry when it's raining cats and dogs.

① You can use more than one adjective to describe a noun. Put all of the adjectives between the article and the noun. Separate the adjectives with a comma.

> One thing I love about Arica is the **clean, fresh** air.
> It was a **hot, muggy** day.
> She has a **big, green, plastic** umbrella.
> The **cold, wet** rain made me feel sick.

② The order of the adjectives depends on the nature of the words. The usual order is: opinion , size , color . If they are the same type of adjective, any order is okay.

> The cute , little , gray mouse ran away.
> It was a hot , uncomfortable day.
> It was an uncomfortable , hot day.

E. Find the mistakes with the multiple adjectives and write the correct sentence.

1. **Incorrect:** I love the blue beautiful water in the Caribbean.

   Correct: _____ I love the beautiful, blue water in the Caribbean. _____

2. **Incorrect:** Have you seen my black suitcase big?

   Correct: _____

3. **Incorrect:** I hate scary, black, big spiders.

   Correct: _____

4. **Incorrect:** There was a cloud big gray in the sky all day.

   Correct: _____

5. **Incorrect:** Have you seen that tree? It has pink, big, beautiful flowers.

   Correct: _____

6. **Incorrect:** The Bananaquit is a yellow, little bird native to the Caribbean.

   Correct: _____

7. **Incorrect:** It was a beautiful day clear.

   Correct: _____

8. **Incorrect:** The Amazon Rainforest has lots of large, unusual bugs.

   Correct: _____

3-1 YES / NO QUESTIONS IN THE PRESENT PERFECT

❶ Yes / no questions in the present perfect ask if something happened at a non-specific time in the past.

> Have you ever studied French?
> Has she ever read *War and Peace?*
> Have they eaten breakfast?

❷ The subject of the sentence goes between *have / has* and the *main verb.* The adverb *ever* is optional, but commonly used.

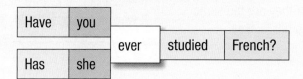

❸ The answer to a Yes / No present perfect question is usually a short answer and also in the present perfect.

> Have you ever been to Canada?
> Have you ever seen *The Titanic?*

> Yes, I have.
> No, I haven't.

REMEMBER

When using the present perfect, the main verb of the sentence should be a past participle.

✓ Have you ever eaten sushi?
✗ Have you ever ate sushi?
✗ Have you ever eat sushi?

A. Write Yes / No questions in the present perfect using the words in parentheses.

1. *Have you ever played* an instrument? *(you / play)*

2. _____ a boy band video? *(you / see)*

3. _____ in Japan? *(he / tour)*

4. _____ an award? *(the Beatles / win)*

5. _____ a reunion tour? *(the Monkees / play)*

6. _____ for a band? *(you / audition)*

7. _____ a new member? *(the Backstreet Boys / get)*

8. _____ more hits that the Beatles? *(anyone / have)*

B. Answer the questions.

1. Have you ever wanted to be a musician? _____

2. Have you ever liked a boy band? _____

3. Has your mother ever told you to turn off your music? _____

4. Has your favorite band ever won an award? _____

❶ *How long* questions ask about the duration of an event that began in the past and continues into the present. It is usually used with the present perfect continuous tense.

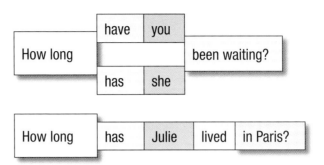

	have	you	
How long			been waiting?
	has	she	

❷ You can also form *How long* questions using the present perfect tense.

How long	has	Julie	lived	in Paris?

❸ Answers to *How long* questions usually have *for* or *since* in them.

I've been waiting **for** twenty minutes.
Julie has lived in Paris **since** 2004.

> **REMEMBER**
>
> Use *for* with a <u>duration of time</u> *(2 years, 3 days, 10 minutes)* and *since* with a <u>specific time in the past</u> *(2005, January, yesterday).*
> ✓ I have been living here *since* <u>May</u>.
> ✓ I have known Paul *for* <u>years</u>.
> ✗ I have been living here ~~*for* 2003~~.
> ✗ I have known Paul ~~*since* 2 months~~.

C. Write *for* or *since* in the blank.

1. I have been a Westlife fan _____ two years.

2. I haven't seen the Backstreet Boys play _____ 2000.

3. Julie has only been listening to her iPod _____ 20 minutes.

4. You have been playing your music too loud _____ hours.

5. The Beatles haven't made an album _____ a long time.

6. Westlife has been around _____ 1999.

7. I've been listening to my new CD _____ five days straight!

8. Boy bands have been topping the charts _____ years.

D. Answer the questions.

1. How long have you been studying English? _____

2. How long have you known your best friend? _____

3. How long has your English teacher worked at your school? _____

4. How long have you been a student at your school? _____

5. How long have you liked your favorite band? _____

Unscramble the *How long* questions.

1. have / How / lived / long / San Jose / you / in / ?

    How long have you lived in San Jose?

2. long / been / for / waiting / you / How / have / me / ?

    _____

3. has / famous / Josh / been / long / How / ?

    _____

4. been / long / sick / has / How / than / your teacher / ?

    _____

5. John Lennon / been / How / dead / has / long / ?

    _____

6. you / N'Sync / How / liked / long / Bill / have / ?

    _____

F. Write *How long* questions using the words below.

1. (she / live / in Chile) _____ *How long has she lived in Chile?* _____

2. (you / be / on vacation) _____

3. (you / own / that book) _____

4. (California / ban / smoking in public) _____

5. (Brad Pitt / be / famous) _____

6. (you / be / alive) _____

7. (Bill Gates / work / at Microsoft) _____

8. (you / know / your teacher) _____

9. (humans / exist) _____

10. (David Beckham/ play / soccer) _____

❶ A *noun clause* can replace a *noun* as the **subject** of the sentence.

His neighborhood is dangerous.

Where he lives is dangerous.

❷ A noun clause can also replace a noun as the **object** of the sentence.

He's a master in creating *boy bands*.

He's a master in creating *what the world calls "boy bands."*

❸ We use **question words** to introduce noun clauses. For example: *how, what, when, where, who, whom.*

What she wore was too casual for the meeting.
I don't know *who* her boyfriend is.
I don't know *where* he went.
When she called was too late.
I know *how* I got here.

REMEMBER

A noun clause should have a subject and verb of its own.

✓ I don't know what she wants.

✗ I don't know what wants.

G. Write the correct question word for each noun clause.

1. I don't know that woman.	I don't know _____ that woman is.
2. I love your dress.	I love _____ you are wearing.
3. I don't know the time.	I don't know _____ time it is.
4. Her house was peaceful.	_____ she lived was peaceful.
5. The instructions for the DVD player were confusing.	_____ to use the DVD player was confusing.
6. He request was too much.	_____ she wanted was too much.
7. I don't know the time of the game.	I don't know _____ the game starts.
8. His school is far away.	_____ he goes to school is far away.
9. The time I should come is unclear.	_____ I should come is unclear.
10. Her house is down the street.	_____ she lives is down the street.

4-1 GERUNDS AS SUBJECTS

❶ A gerund is a verb + –*ing,* for example, *working.* A gerund works like a noun. You can use a gerund as a subject or object in a sentence.

Avoiding unpleasant tasks is easy to do.
Multitasking is important in the work world.
She enjoys **reading** at night.

❷ Gerunds are singular. The verb in the sentence should agree with the gerund. But two or more subject gerunds require a plural verb.

Learning to set priorities **is** difficult for many people.
Skiing, cooking, and **writing** poetry **are** her hobbies.

❸ You can use gerunds as subjects with any verb tense.

Opening my own restaurant **was** the best thing I ever did.
Wasting time **has been** my biggest mistake.

A. Finish the sentences using gerunds as subjects.

1. _____ is easy.

2. _____ was the hardest thing I've ever done.

3. _____ is one of my favorite things to do.

4. _____ has been my biggest mistake in life.

5. _____ is fun, but _____ is even better.

6. _____ was one of the best parts about being a child.

B. Finish the sentences about the following activities.

1. Multitasking _____.

2. Setting priorities and working hard _____.

3. Worrying _____.

4. Procrastinating _____.

5. Failing _____.

6. Wasting time _____.

4-2 GERUNDS IN PREPOSITIONAL PHRASES

1 Gerunds can be used as objects in prepositional phrases.

> Thank you **for driving** me to the airport.
> I am capable **of working** in the corporate world.
> She is thinking **about going** back to school.

2 Put *not* before a gerund to make it negative.

> Jack is afraid of **not having** enough money to support his family.

> She is thinking about **not going** back to school.

C. Unscramble the prepositional phrases to finish each sentence.

1. great / accomplishing / of / things / many / .

   She is capable ___of accomplishing many great things.___

2. my / about / office / organizing /.

   I was thinking _____

3. tasks / unpleasant / at / avoiding /.

   He was good _____

4. not / where / begin / knowing / to / of / .

   I am afraid _____

5. room / cleaning / for / your / .

   Thank you _____

6. delegating / to / his employees / work / of / not / .

   He is guilty _____

7. doing / many / of / at once / things / .

   Jan was capable _____

8. homework / doing / of / tonight / not / his / .

   Charles is thinking _____

9. not / successful / being / of / .

   I had been afraid _____

4-3 VERBS FOLLOWED BY GERUNDS

❶ Some verbs can be followed by gerunds. In these sentences, the gerund is the object of the verb.

> I **avoid watching** T.V. as much as possible.
> She **appreciates hearing** from you.

❷ These verbs are followed by gerunds regardless of the verb tense of the sentence.

> I **delayed talking** to my professor.
> He **is considering moving** to Costa Rica.
> I **have finished writing** my paper.

❸ The gerund and following phrases can be replaced by a pronoun.

> I don't **mind helping you**.
>
> I don't **mind it**.

REMEMBER

Common verbs that are followed by gerunds:

appreciate

avoid

consider

delay

finish

mind

✓ I avoid talking to him.

✗ I avoid ~~to talk~~ to him.

✗ I avoid ~~talk~~ to him.

D. Find the mistakes and write the correct sentence.

1. **Incorrect:** I finished do my homework.

   Correct: _____I finished doing my homework._____

2. **Incorrect:** She delayed to going on her vacation.

   Correct: _____

3. **Incorrect:** I am avoiding cleaning it my office.

   Correct: _____

4. **Incorrect:** I don't mind to listen to your problems.

   Correct: _____

5. **Incorrect:** I appreciate to knowing how you feel.

   Correct: _____

E. Use gerunds to finish the sentences about you.

1. I avoid _____

2. I don't mind _____

3. I haven't finished _____

4. I am considering _____

5. I appreciate _____

❶ *Go* is followed by a **gerund** when talking about recreational activities.

> They **go hiking** in Colorado every summer.
> I **went sledding** with my younger brother last week.
> Greg **will go running** after school if it doesn't rain
> I **haven't gone fishing** in years.

❷ A gerund following *go* cannot be replaced by a pronoun, but you can replace *go* + gerund with *do* + pronoun.

> Greg **goes camping** every summer.
> ✗ Greg ~~goes it~~ every summer.
> ✓ Greg **does it** every summer.
>
> Rose **goes skiing** every winter.
> She **does it** every winter.

F. For each statement write *true* or *false* for you. If it's *false*, write a true sentence.

Statement	True or False?	True Statement about You
1. I am going camping next weekend.		
2. I haven't gone sledding in years.		
3. I want to go skating next winter.		
4. I went dancing last weekend.		
5. I won't go hiking in the mountains.		
6. I have never gone canoeing.		

G. Write sentences about recreational activities that you enjoy or don't enjoy. Use *go* + gerund.

1. _____

2. _____

3. _____

5-1 PHRASAL MODAL VERBS

1 Phrasal modals have multiple words and end in the word *to*. They have meanings very similar to their corresponding modal.

Modal	Phrasal Modal
can	be able to
will	be going to
must	have to
should	be supposed to

2 The verb in the phrasal modal agrees with the subject of the sentence. The main verb comes after the phrasal modal and is in the simple form.

> She **is supposed to** have her dog on a leash.
> Watch out! The dog **is going to** jump on you!
> Many birds **have to** fly south in the winter because they cannot survive in the cold weather.

3 Change the verb tense of the phrasal modal to talk about different time periods.

> I **was supposed to** get a pet fish, I but got a cat instead.
> I **haven't been able to** find my cat anywhere.

A. Rewrite the sentences changing the modals to phrasal modals.

1. Chickens can't fly.

   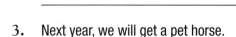
   Chickens are not able to fly.

2. You should feed your pet every day.

   _____

3. Next year, we will get a pet horse.

   _____

4. You must take your dog on a walk.

   _____

5. I'm allergic to cats so I won't get one.

   _____

6. Whales must live in the ocean.

   _____

7. I won't get a pet until I'm older.

   _____

8. You shouldn't get a pet if you don't have time to take care of it.

   _____

5-2 MODALS AND PHRASAL MODALS OF NECESSITY

1 We use *must* to talk about very strong necessity, such as laws and rules.

> All pets **must** be registered at the front desk.
> Dogs **must** be on a leash.

2 We use *have to* to talk about ordinary necessity.

> I **have to** buy food for my pet bird tonight.
> When we had a dog, we **had to** take it for a walk five times a day.

3 We use *had to* when talking about a necessity in the past.

> I **had to** get a leash for my dog.
> Barbara **had to** take her dog for a walk.

B. Finish the sentences.

1. Today I must _____

2. My teacher had to _____

3. My friends have to _____

4. All students must _____

5. Yesterday I had to _____

6. My mother must _____

7. Before I could drive a car, I had to _____

8. When I was a child I had to _____

9. When my father was a child he had to _____

10. All people going on an airplane must _____

11. Before I graduate, I have to _____

12. All weapons must _____

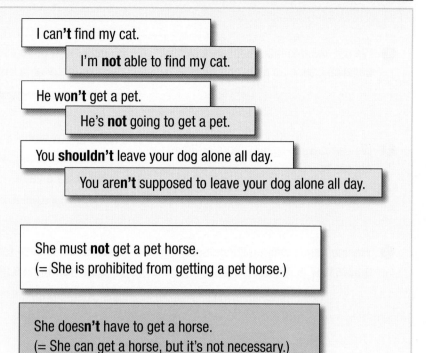

① Most modals and phrasal modals have the **same meaning** as one another when you add *not*.

I can**'t** find my cat.

I'm **not** able to find my cat.

He won**'t** get a pet.

He's **not** going to get a pet.

You **shouldn't** leave your dog alone all day.

You are**n't** supposed to leave your dog alone all day.

② *Must* and *have to* have **different meanings** when you add *not*.

She must **not** get a pet horse.
(= She is prohibited from getting a pet horse.)

She does**n't** have to get a horse.
(= She can get a horse, but it's not necessary.)

C. For each situation, write a sentence using a negative modal or phrasal modal.

1. You can feed your cat on your lunch break, but it's not necessary.

   I don't have to feed my cat on my lunch break.

2. Your friend is hitting his dog. You want to tell him that this is a bad thing to do.

   _____

3. Bob is prohibited from playing with the Seeing Eye dog.

   _____

4. Your friend is scared that your dog will bite him. You know the dog will not do this.

   _____

5. Julie is able to pet the cat, but it's not necessary.

   _____

6. You want to train your horse, but you don't know enough about horses.

   _____

7. Owners are prohibited from bringing their pets into the store.

   _____

❶ Although *can* and *be able to* have the same meaning, *can* is less formal and commonly used in spoken language. *Be able to* is more formal and commonly used in written language.

> Basilisk lizards *can* run on water. (less formal)
> Basilisk lizards *are able* to run on water. (more formal)

❷ *Can* cannot be used in these types of sentences, so *be able to* must be used:
- with other modals
- with the perfect tense
- with gerunds, participles and infinitives

> - You **should** *be able to* take care of your pet.
> - For years, my dog ***has been*** *able to* sense when I'm coming home.
> - ***Being*** *able to* run on water is unusual.

D. For each sentence, decide if you can use *can* in place of *be able to*. If you can use it, write the sentence below. If you can't use it, check the box.

Cannot use *can*

1. I might be able to get a dog next year if my parents say it's okay.

   _____   ☑

2. Many animals are able to sense when there is going to be bad weather.

   Many animals can sense when there is going to be bad weather.   ☐

3. Moles aren't able to see in the light.

   _____   ☐

4. Being able to fly is lucky.

   _____   ☐

5. Some snakes are able to climb trees.

   _____   ☐

6. I haven't been able to get a dog because I travel so much.

   _____   ☐

7. My pet bird is able to hear noises that I can't hear.

   _____   ☐

8. I think people shouldn't be able to take their dogs into hotel rooms.

   _____   ☐

6-1 ADJECTIVE CLAUSES WITH TIME

❶ Use *when* in an adjective clause that talks about a time (time, day, month, year, etc.)

> Early morning is the time **when I dream the most.**
> December is the month **when I have the most stress.**

❷ You can replace *when* with *in / on which* or *that.* When used to introduce adjective clauses, these words are called relative pronouns.

> Early morning is the time **that I dream the most.**
> December is the month **in which I have the most stress.**

❸ You can leave out *when* and the sentence has the same meaning.

> Early morning is the time **I dream the most.**
> December is the month **I have the most stress.**

A. Read the sentences and correct the mistakes. Some of the sentences are correct.

1. Thursday is the day in when I have the busiest schedule.

   Thursday is the day when I have the busiest schedule.

2. 2 P.M. is when the time I need a cup of coffee.

   _____

3. February is the month which I most need a vacation.

   _____

4. Midnight is the time when that I get very tired.

   _____

5. Halloween is the holiday when I eat the most candy.

   _____

6. Tomorrow is the day in I have to stay late at work.

   _____

7. 8 A.M. is the time in that I go to school.

   _____

8. October is the month it starts to get cold.

   _____

❶ Use *where* in an adjective clause that talks about a place (country, city, specific building, etc.).

> The meadow **where I saw the cow** was full of flowers.
> The church **where we got married** is over there.

❷ You can replace *where* with *which* or *that*, but you have to add the preposition *in* to the sentence.

> The meadow **that I saw the cow in** was full of flowers.
> The church **in which we got married** is over there.

❸ You can leave out *where* entirely if you add the preposition *in* at the end of the adjective clause.

> The meadow **I saw the cow in** was full of flowers.
> The church **we got married in** is over there.

REMEMBER

When *which* or *that* is the object of a preposition, there are four ways to form the adjective clause.

The house **that I grew up in** is on this street. (informal)
The house **which I grew up in** is on this street. (informal)
The house **I grew up in** is on this street. (informal)
The house **in which I grew up** is on this street. (formal)

B. Rewrite each sentence using the relative pronoun in parentheses. Ø = *no relative pronoun*.

1. *(that)* The house where I grew up is often in my dreams.

    _____*The house that I grew up in is often in my dreams.*_____

2. *(Ø)* The school where I studied as a child seems smaller now.

    _____

3. *(which)* The neighborhood where I used to play was very nice.

    _____

4. *(where)* The house that my mother grew up in is very old.

    _____

5. *(which)* The room where I slept was very messy.

    _____

6. *(where)* The cage my pet hamster lived in had lots of toys.

    _____

7. *(Ø)* The playground where I used to play is now a parking garage.

    _____

8. *(that)* The house where my friend lived is now painted blue.

    _____

6-3 ADJECTIVE CLAUSES WITH POSSESSIVES

❶ When using adjective clauses within a sentence, use *whose* to replace the possessive adjectives *my, your, our, his, her, its,* and *their*.

> The author is over there. I'm reading **his** book.
> > The author **whose** book I'm reading is over there.

> The girl is shy. **Her** dreams were analyzed.
> > The girl **whose** dreams were analyzed is shy.

❷ *Whose* always comes at the beginning of the adjective clause, before the noun.

> The boy **whose** father is my doctor just came in.
> The writer **whose** work I admire most is Jane Austen.

C. Rewrite the sentences into one sentence using adjective clauses with possessives.

1. The man is wearing a black hat. His daughter got into Harvard University.

    The man whose daughter got into Harvard University is wearing a black hat.

2. The woman is walking in right now. Her book has just been published.

    _____

3. The girl is creative. Her painting won the art award.

    _____

4. The man is very happy. His daughter won the award for music.

    _____

5. The boy has on a blue sweater. His paper got an A+.

    _____

6. The girl is wearing glasses. Her science project won first prize.

    _____

7. The woman is clapping and cheering. Her son just got his diploma.

    _____

8. The boy is going to give a speech. His scholarship was just announced.

    _____

1 You can reduce an adjective clause to an adjective phrase. For continuous sentences, leave out the relative pronoun and the verb *be*.

> The woman ~~who was~~ talking about her recurring dreams is my grandmother.

2 For sentences in the present or past that have *be* as the main verb, leave out the relative pronoun and the verb *be*.

> The book ~~that is~~ about dreams was written by my uncle.

3 For present tense sentences with other verbs, you can sometimes leave out the relative pronoun and change the verb to the *–ing* form.

> involving
>
> Dreams ~~that involve~~ falling can be frightening.

REMEMBER

You cannot reduce adjective clauses if the relative pronoun is the object of the sentence.
✓ The man ~~who is~~ sitting over there won the lottery.
✗ The man ~~who I was~~ talking to won the lottery.

D. In the following sentences, reduce the adjective clauses to adjective phrases. In one of the sentences, the adjective clause cannot be reduced.

1. The travel guide that is on Costa Rica is excellent.

    _____ *The travel guide on Costa Rica is excellent.* _____

2. The boy that we are going to travel with is named Rob.

    _____

3. The T.V. show that is about traveling in Costa Rica starts in an hour.

    _____

4. All planes that were leaving Seoul were delayed because of snow.

    _____

Villa Caletas, Costa Rica

5. Dreams that take place in another time and place are very interesting.

    _____

6. The girl who was showing us her pictures from Italy just went back last week.

    _____

7. The flight that goes from New York to Tokyo is very exhausting.

    _____

8. Nightmares that involve packing are very frustrating.

    _____

7-1 USING *COULD* AND *MIGHT* IN PRESENT UNREAL CONDITIONALS

❶ You can use *could* or *might* instead of *would* in present unreal conditional sentences. Use *might* to express uncertainty and *could* to express ability.

If I had the money, I **might** go.
If I didn't have a test tomorrow, I **could** go to the movies with you tonight.
If your boss wasn't unethical, you **might** feel comfortable around him

❷ You can use *could* in the *if* clause of a present unreal conditional sentence. Use it to express ability to do something.

If I **could ski,** I would go to Switzerland with you.
If you **could meet** any famous person, who would you meet?
If I **could visit** any country in the world, I would go to Nepal.

A. Finish the present unreal conditional sentences using *could* and *might*.

1. If I knew my friend were lying to her parents, _____

2. If I didn't have to study for English class, _____

3. If I found out someone was eavesdropping on my conversations, _____

   _____

4. If I could meet any famous person, _____

5. _____, I might tell the teacher.

6. If I accidentally hurt someone's feelings, _____

7. If I could fly, _____

8. If I could be doing anything else right now, _____

9. If I had more time, _____

10. If I were rich and famous, _____

11. If I had super powers, _____

12. If I could _____, _____

❶ You can use continuous verbs in present unreal conditional sentences.

> If I **were not working** right now, I would be helping my sister move.

❷ Continuous verbs can be used in both clauses of the sentence or in just one of the clauses.

> If it **were snowing,** I wouldn't have to go to school today.
> If Kara were not sick, she **would be working** at the school.
> If Dad were here today, he **would be writing** another book.

REMEMBER

Careful speakers use *were* instead of *was* in the *if* clause of a present unreal conditional sentence

✓ If she **were** here, I'd be happy.

✓ If she **was** here, I'd be happy.

B. Finish the present unreal conditional sentences using the continuous form of the verbs in parentheses when appropriate.

1. If my back (hurt / not) _weren't hurting_, I would (move) _move_ those boxes.

2. If I (have) _____ the money, I would (buy) _____ that dress.

3. If it (rain / not) _____, we could (go) _____ to the beach.

4. If I (be / not) _____ busy right now, I could (come) _____with you.

5. If she (feel / not) _____ sick, she would (go) _____ out tonight.

6. If we (fight / not) _____, I could (call) _____ her for help.

7. If she (sleep) _____ right now, she would (feel) _____ rested later.

8. If I (live) _____ in a city, I might (earn) _____ more money.

9. If she (be/not) _____ sick, she would (write) _____ the book.

10. If it (be/not) _____ warm today, I would (wear) _____ a t-shirt.

11. If I (know) _____ her phone number, I could (talk) _____ to her.

12. If I (live) _____ closer to my family, they might (visit) _____ me.

7-3 VERBS + INFINITIVE

❶ Some verbs may be followed by an infinitive.

> I **decided to tell** the truth.
> She **forgot to invite** Tony to the party.

❷ Some verbs may be followed by a an object + an infinitive.

> Sarah **convinced me to tell** her my secret.
> Susan **persuaded John to be** unethical.

❸ Some verbs may be followed by either an infinitive or by an object + an infinitive.

> I **want to win** the prize
> I **want him to win** the prize.

❹ For both types of verbs, we put *not* before the infinitive to make a negative.

> I decided **not to gossip** anymore.
> Carrie begged me **not to tell** anyone her secret.

REMEMBER

Verb + Infinitive	Verbs + Object + Infinitive	Verb + Infinitive OR Verb + Object + Infinitive
agree	allow	beg
decide	convince	expect
forget	encourage	want
hope	forbid	
intend	invite	
offer	persuade	
plan	require	
pretend		
promise		

C. Unscramble the sentences.

1. her / I / to tell / encouraged / truth / the /.

   I encouraged her to tell the truth.

2. to / to go / party / She / the / intends /.

   _____

3. her / He / the / agreed / money / to pay /.

   _____

4. to hide / expected / the / him / truth / I /.

   _____

5. convinced / to stop / cheating / Bill / I /. _____

6. again / to eavesdrop / promised / Susan / not / ever /. _____

7. forbids / to tell / me / mother / lies / My / white /. _____

8. to pay / back / him / offered / I /. _____

9. him / Jude / not / to act / convinced / unethically /. _____

In passive sentences with verb + object + infinitive, the object pronoun or noun becomes the subject.

Active: Terry persuaded **me** to eavesdrop on Jeff's conversation.
Passive: I was persuaded to eavesdrop on Jeff's conversation.

Active: I invited **Pamela** to go to the party, but she never responded.
Passive: Pamela was invited to go to the party, but she never responded.

D. Rewrite the sentences in the passive voice.

1. She begged me to tell her my secret.

   I was begged to tell my secret.

2. They expected me to be honest.

   _____

3. My father forbids me to eavesdrop on other people's conversations.

   _____

4. She convinced me not to help him.

   _____

5. She persuaded me to tell Julie the truth.

   _____

6. They allowed me to hear the details of what happened.

   _____

7. He invited me to go to his house for dinner.

   _____

8. My parents required me to get good grades.

   _____

9. He begged me to help him with his problem.

   _____

8-1 YES / NO QUESTIONS IN THE PAST PERFECT

❶ You can ask questions in the past perfect. They are usually used to clarify a story being told in the past tense. The past perfect is used to talk about what happened before another time in the past.

> **Ann:** Last night I got home and made dinner. Then I remembered I was supposed to go out to dinner with Jerry.
> **Bob:** Oh, no! **Had you already eaten** dinner before you remembered you were going out?
> **Ann:** No, I hadn't. I put all the food in the refrigerator. I'll eat it tomorrow for lunch.

❷ Form questions in the past perfect with *had* + subject + past participle.

> **Had you tried** to call him before he arrived?
> **Had Tom looked** in the fridge before he ordered a pizza?
> **Had your parents known** each other long before they got married?

A. Find the mistakes with the past perfect questions and write the correct sentence.

1. **Incorrect:** Have you known Bill long before he asked you to get married?

   Correct: _Had you known Bill long before he asked you to get married?_

2. **Incorrect:** Had you date many other guys before you met Bill?

   Correct: _____

3. **Incorrect:** Had Bill dated other girls before he had met you?

   Correct: _____

4. **Incorrect:** Did Tom already bought the ring before you agreed to marry him?

   Correct: _____

5. **Incorrect:** Have you been engaged a long time before you had the wedding?

   Correct: _____

6. **Incorrect:** Did you been married long before you decided to have children?

   Correct: _____

❶ You can ask information questions in the past perfect with *where, why, what, who, how,* and *when.*

> **What had you done** by the time you started getting dressed?
> **Who had your mother expected** you to marry before you met your husband?

❷ When using the past perfect, we often use words like *before, by,* and *since* to refer to another time in the past.

> How many times had you called **before** she answered the phone?
> What had she eaten **since** she got home?

B. Circle the correct answer to complete each question.

1. (What / Where) had you done by the time you left for school?

2. Where (have / had) you gone before your friends arrived?

3. Why (hadn't you tried / didn't you try) to call him before you went out?

4. What had you done before you (heard / had heard) he was sick?

5. When (have / had) you visited him before he moved?

6. How many times had you told him to stay home (before / after) he agreed?

C. Unscramble the questions.

1. had you lived / you moved / Where / to Cleveland / before / ?

   _____

2. by the time / her / How many times / he finally wrote / her e-mail / had she checked / ?

   _____

3. before / Who / that time / had been / your boss / ?

   _____

4. by the time / had he eaten / him / How many pieces of cake / finally stopped / his mother / ?

   _____

5. to finish your homework / you left / hadn't you tried / before / Why / ?

   _____

6. the house / he left / What / before / had Jack said / ?

   _____

❶ Form questions in the past perfect continuous tense with *had* + subject + *been* + verb + *–ing*.

> **Had your mother and father been dating** long before they decided to get married?
> **Why had your mother been living** in England before she married your father?

❷ The most common information questions in the past perfect continuous ask *How long…?* Use them to ask about the duration of an activity in the past that happened before another activity in the past.

> **How long** *had* your mother and father *been dating* before they decided to get married?
> **How long** *had* you *been planning* the party before it got cancelled?

D. Match the first half of the question with the ending that fits best.

1. _____ How long had he been living in China   a. before you saw me?

2. _____ Where had she been working   b. before you realized it was wrong?

3. _____ Had you been looking long   c. before he moved back to Thailand?

4. _____ How long had you been sleeping   d. before you finally told him?

5. _____ What number had you been calling   e. before he woke you up?

6. _____ Had you been planning to tell me   f. before she got the job here?

7. _____ How long had Martha been traveling   g. before I figured it out on my own?

8. _____ How long had you known the truth   h. before she lost her passport?

E. Complete the conversations using the past perfect, past perfect continuous, or simple past of the verbs in parentheses.

Carla: How's the wedding planning going?

Andrea: Actually, it's been complicated. We (decide) _____
                                                                                1

to move the wedding to my hometown in California.

Carla: Where (think) _____ you _____ of having the wedding
                              2   3

before you moved it to California?

Andrea: Originally, we (intend) _____ to have the wedding in Hawaii, but my mother-in-law said
                                              4

it would be too difficult for the family to travel there.

Carla: How long (plan) _____ you _____ the wedding in Hawaii before you moved
                                5   6

it to California?

Andrea: About six months.

Carla: That's a long time. Why (tell / not) _____ she _____ you before you did so much work?
                                                         7   8

Andrea: That's a good question! I hadn't thought of that before now.

Jim: How's school going?

Josh: Pretty good. I (decide) _____ to change my major to business.
                                        1

Jim: What (study) _____ you _____ before you changed your major?
                          2   3

Josh: Philosophy.

Jim: That's interesting. But why (decide) _____ you _____ to change?
                                                    4   5

Josh: I don't know what kind of job I can get with a philosophy degree.

Jim: That's true. How long (major) _____ you _____ in philosophy
                                            6   7

before you (decide) _____ to change your major to business?
                            8

Josh: About a year.

Maria: Hi, Tom! What happened to your arm?

Tom: I (get) _____ in a car accident last week. I was driving and I fell asleep.
                    1

Maria: Oh no! How long (drive) _____ you _____ _____ before you got in the accident?
                                      2   3   4

Tom: Only 20 minutes, but, I (sleep/not) _____ _____ in over 24 hours.
                                                  5   6

Maria: Why hadn't you slept in so long?

Tom: Because I (study) _____ _____ _____ for a big English test.
                              7   8   9

Maria: That's terrible. (get) _____ you _____ a good grade on the test?
                                    10   11

Tom: Yeah! I got an A!

Unit 9

9-1 PRESENT PERFECT IN REPORTED SPEECH

Direct Speech: "I **have done** it," Mike said.

Indirect Speech: Mike said he **had done** it.

❶ We use the past perfect to report direct speech in the present perfect.

Direct Speech: "He **has interrupted** me many times," Mary said.

Indirect Speech: Mary said he **had interrupted** her many times.

❷ As with reported speech in other tenses, no quotation marks are used and the subject pronouns are changed to reflect the speaker.

Direct Speech: She said, "I have lived in Seoul for five years."

Indirect Speech: She said **she** had lived in Seoul for five years.

A. Rewrite the sentences in reported speech.

1. Milena said, "I have tried to be assertive at work for years."

   Milena said she had tried to be assertive at work for years.

2. Jonathan said, "I have always been direct with you."

   _____

3. Mike said, "She has ignored my feelings too many times."

   _____

4. Chris said, "I have never understood women."

   _____

5. Ann said, "Mike has always been too sensitive."

   _____

6. Phyllis said, "I have tried to interrupt him, but he has never let me."

   _____

7. Wade said, "I have never been too blunt."

   _____

1 Some modals change to other modals in reported speech.

Direct Speech	Reported Speech
will	would
can	could
may	might

He said, "I **can**'t change my communication style."

He said he **could**n't change his communication style.

2 Some modals stay the same in reported speech.

Direct Speech	Reported Speech
should	should
might	might

"You **should** be direct," my boss said.

My boss said I **should** be more direct.

3 *Must* changes to *had to* in reported speech.

"I **must** go home," she said.

She said she **had to** go home.

4 Phrasal modals change from present to past tense in reported speech.

Direct Speech	Reported Speech
am / is going to	was going to
are going to	were going to
have / has to	had to

Lee said, "Bob **is going to** get a new computer."

Lee said Bob **was going to** get a new computer.

B. Match the sentences in direct speech with their equivalent in reported speech.

Direct Speech	Reported Speech
1. _____ She said, "I can come tonight."	a. She said she wasn't going to come tonight.
2. _____ She said, "I'm not going to come tonight."	b. She said she would come tonight.
3. _____ She said, "I may come tonight."	c. She said she couldn't come tonight.
4. _____ She said, "I won't come tonight."	d. She said she was going to come tonight.
5. _____ She said, "I have to come tonight."	e. She said she could come tonight.
6. _____ She said, "I will come tonight."	f. She said she had to come tonight.
7. _____ She said, "I can't come tonight."	g. She said she might not come tonight.
8. _____ She said, "I might not come tonight."	h. She said she might come tonight.
9. _____ She said, "I am going to come tonight."	i. She said she wouldn't come tonight.

❶ We can use reported speech in questions. Change the subject and verb in the direct speech to the statement form.

> She said, "**Do you like** this crisp weather?"
>
> > She asked if **I liked** this crisp weather.

❷ Add the word *if* before the statement.

> Barb said, "Is Janet taking this course?"
>
> > Barb asked **if** Janet was taking this course.

❸ Make these verb tense changes in reported speech.

> He said, "**Did** you **lose** your cell phone?"
>
> > He asked if I **had lost** my cell phone.

Direct Speech	Reported Speech
present tense	past tense
simple past	past perfect
present continuous	past continuous

C. Unscramble the reported speech sentences.

1. I / if / She / wanted / more / asked / go / to /.

   _____

2. asked / the baby / Sharon / had / he / if / fed /.

   _____

3. he / Jason / come in / asked / could / if /.

   _____

4. she / called / if / Charlie / had / him / asked /.

   _____

5. if / asked / was / tonight / coming / Bill / He /.

   _____

6. me / Elise / the / knew / I / if / asked / time /.

   _____

7. if / Nathan / I / to / asked / wanted / me / sit down.

   _____

8. asked / had / he / dinner / Tina / if / eaten / yet /.

   _____

9-4 *TO BE* QUESTIONS IN REPORTED SPEECH

❶ To change a *to be* question to reported speech, change the question to a statement.

> Barry said, "**Are you** cold?"
>> Barry asked if **I was** cold.

❷ Add *if* before the statement.

> Greg said, "Are your co-workers nice?"
>> Greg asked **if** my co-workers were nice.

❸ *To be* verbs follow the same rules for changing.

Direct Speech	Reported Speech
am/is	was
are	were
was/were	had been

> She said, "**Was** I too blunt?"
>> She asked if she **had been** too blunt.

D. Rewrite the sentences as reported speech.

1. Chad said, "Are you tired today?"

   Chad asked if I was tired today.

2. Carol said, "Were there too many people in the class?"

3. Sara said, "Were you home last night?"

4. She said, "Am I too direct?"

5. She said, "Do you think women are more talkative than men?"

6. Kevin said, "Was it too hot in the room yesterday?"

7. He said, "Is my communication style too blunt?"

8. Shannon said, "Are you generally a good sleeper?"

Unit 10

10-1 USING CONTINUOUS VERBS WITH CONDITIONALS

❶ Use continuous verbs in the **present** unreal conditional to show the duration of an event. Use past continuous with *were*.

> If he **were** not **sleeping** right now, we *could* ask him.
> If I **were sitting** at my desk, I *would* be bored.

❷ You can also use continuous verbs in the **past** unreal conditional. Use past perfect continuous.

> If it **had** not **been snowing**, I *wouldn't have gotten* in a car accident.
> I *would have passed* the test if I **had been listening** in class.

A. Complete the conditional sentences using the past continuous or past perfect continuous form of the verb in parenthesis.

1. If I (sleep/not) _____, I would have heard you come in.

2. If you (work) _____, you would have the money to live.

3. If it (rain/not) _____, I wouldn't have ruined my shoes.

4. If you (pay) _____ attention, you would have gotten a better grade.

5. If I (feel) _____ optimistic, I would tell you it will all be okay.

6. If it (snow/not) _____ so much, we could drive there.

7. If you (act/not) _____ so impatient, I would have asked you for help.

8. If I (be/not) _____ so stubborn, I could have helped him.

9. If you (watch/not) _____ TV right now, you could (get) _____ a lot of work done.

10. If you (listen) _____ to me, you would know why I was so upset.

11. If he (feel) _____ rattled, it would be obvious.

12. If Anne (cook) _____ dinner, I would be very happy.

10-2 CONDITIONALS WITHOUT *IF*

❶ You can leave out *if* in present unreal conditional sentences that use *were*. *Were* comes before the subject of the sentence.

> **Were I** optimistic, I would tell you everything is going to be okay.
> I would have worn my new coat **were it** cold today.

❷ You can also leave out *if* in past unreal conditional sentences. *Had* comes before the subject.

> **Had** the directions **been** clearer, Evan could have figured our how to program the DVR.
> **Had** the subway **not broken down**, George might have arrived on time.

❸ In both types of sentences, *not* goes after the subject.

> **Were** you **not** so busy all the time, we could go to dinner together.
> **Had** George **not been** late, he might have gotten the job.

REMEMBER

You cannot leave out *if* in present unreal conditional sentences unless the main verb is *be*.

✓ Were he more flexible, he would be successful.

✗ ~~Saw I~~ a rainbow, I would tell you.

B. Rewrite each conditional sentence without *if.* For sentences where *if* cannot be left out, write Ø.

1. If Ken were trustworthy, I would ask him to walk my dog.

   Were Ken trustworthy, I would ask him to walk my dog.

2. If you had been on time, you wouldn't have missed the beginning.

   _____

3. If Claire had not screamed at the meeting, she might have been invited back.

   _____

4. If you hadn't been so impatient, you would have made a better impression.

   _____

5. If you weren't so honest, you wouldn't be as successful as you are today.

   _____

6. If I knew the answer, I would tell you.

   _____

7. If you were a flexible person, you would be willing to change your plans.

   _____

8. If I had been more easygoing, I might have gotten the job.

   _____

10-3 REVIEW OF CONDITIONALS

① Real conditional sentences in the present are used for habitual action or general truths. Use present tense in both clauses.

> If I **get** frustrated at work, I **take** a break.

② Real conditional sentences in the future use present tense in the *if* clause and future tense in the result clause.

> If my car **breaks** down, I **will call** you for a ride.

③ Unreal conditional sentences in the present use simple past in the *if* clause and *would* + simple verb in the result clause.

> If Carla **were**n't so trustworthy, I **would**n't **ask** her for help.

④ Past unreal conditional sentences use the past perfect in the *if* clause and *would have* + past participle in the result clause.

> If George **had been** more organized, he **would have arrived** on time for the interview.

C. Match the first half of each sentence to its correct ending.

1. _____ If you get the job,

2. _____ If she had arrived to work on time everyday,

3. _____ If I get a lot of work done in a day,

4. _____ If I have time,

5. _____ If I had the power to make changes in my office,

6. _____ If my boss weren't so temperamental,

7. _____ If we had needed to hire two people,

8. _____ If Bob gets a raise,

a. we would have offered you a position.

b. I reward myself by getting a massage.

c. people wouldn't be quitting.

d. I would hire many new people.

e. I will throw a party for you.

f. he won't look for a new job.

g. I go to the gym after work.

h. she wouldn't have gotten fired.

D. Circle the correct verb in each sentence.

1. If Julia (hadn't been / weren't) so self-centered, she would have more friends.

2. If I ever see Peter again, I (will / would) tell him the truth.

3. If you freeze water, it (turns / had turned) to ice.

4. If her friends (live / lived) nearby, she wouldn't be calling me so often.

5. If you had gone to bed earlier last night, you (would have felt / will feel) rested today.

6. If you (bother / bothered) me again, I will get rattled.

7. If I could live anywhere in the world, I (live / would live) in Brazil.

8. If it (rains / rained) tomorrow, I will be very disappointed.

9. If I (hadn't been / wasn't) so busy when you were in town, I could have seen you.

10. If I have extra money, I (would put / put) it in the bank.

E. Finish the conditional sentences.

1. If there were world peace, _____

2. If I have time tomorrow, _____

3. I wouldn't have been upset _____

4. My parents would have disowned me _____

5. If you put a lot of pressure on me, _____

6. If my teacher stopped giving us homework, _____

7. If I had known then what I know now, _____

8. My family will be very proud of me _____

9. I would throw a big party _____

10. If I had had the time, _____

11-1 WISHES FOR THE FUTURE

❶ We can make wishes for the future using *were going to* + simple verb.

> I wish John **were going to go** to dinner tonight.
> I wish I **were going to get** home earlier.

❷ You can also use *wish* with the structure *would* + simple verb to make wishes for the future.

> I wish Helen **would come** to the party with us.
> I wish Reed **wouldn't go** out tonight.

❸ *I wish you would* + simple verb is sometimes used to make requests.

> I **wish you would turn off** the light.
> I **wish you would tell** me where you were all day.
> I **wish you wouldn't call** me Mrs. Jones. Just call me Barb.

A. Find the mistakes and write the correct sentence.

1. **Incorrect:** I wish Tina is going to come on vacation with us.

    Correct: *I wish Tina were going to come on vacation with us.*

2. **Incorrect:** I wish you make that delicious chocolate cake for me.

    Correct: _____

3. **Incorrect:** I wish you don't would play your music so loud.

    Correct: _____

4. **Incorrect:** I wish would Bob go to the doctor.

    Correct: _____

5. **Incorrect:** I wish I were going finish my paper tonight.

    Correct: _____

6. **Incorrect:** I wish you was going to go to the festival tomorrow.

    Correct: _____

7. **Incorrect:** She wish her mother were going to be there.

    Correct: _____

8. **Incorrect:** He wishes the war would ends.

    Correct: _____

B. Write a request for each situation.

1. It's very cold in here because the window is open.

   I wish you would close the window.

2. I'm tired and want to go to sleep. The T.V. is on and it's keeping me up.

   _____

3. I'm thirsty, but I don't want to get up.

   _____

4. I don't like the show on T.V. There's a good show on another channel.

   _____

5. The dinner you cooked is good, but there's too much salt in it.

   _____

6. You live far away, and you don't come to visit enough.

   _____

C. Write 8 wishes for the future.

1. _____
2. _____
3. _____
4. _____
5. _____
6. _____
7. _____
8. _____

> ❶ In present or future sentences with *wish*, we use *could* + simple verb to talk about ability.

> **Present**
> I wish I **could speak** French.
> She wishes she **could solve** the math problem.
>
> **Future**
> I wish he **could come** to our house tomorrow.
> He wishes he **could go** out tonight, but he can't.

D. Circle the correct words to finish the sentences.

1. I wish I could (go / have gone) home, but I have to stay at work.

2. Kathleen wishes she could (knit / knitted).

3. Mel wishes he could (see / seen) the movie tonight.

4. I wish I could (see / seeing) you tonight.

5. I wish you could (come / came) tomorrow.

6. Carla wishes she could (cook / cooking).

7. I wish I could (go / will go) to Japan next year.

8. I wish you could (stay / stayed) at the party.

E. Finish the sentences about <u>you</u> using *could* + simple verb.

1. I wish _____.

2. I wish _____ tomorrow.

3. I wish _____ when I was a child.

4. I wish _____ some day.

5. I wish _____ next year.

6. I wish _____.

❶ You can use continuous verbs in statements with *wish* about present situations. Use the structure *were* + verb + *–ing*.

> I wish I **were sleeping** right now.
> She wishes they **were waiting** for her.
> He wishes it **weren't snowing** today.
> I wish it **weren't getting** so late.

❷ Past situations with *wish* that require the continuous verb form use the structure *had been* + verb + *–ing*.

> I wish I **had been listening** earlier.
> She wishes he **had been waiting** for her.
> He wishes it **hadn't been snowing** yesterday.
> I wish we **hadn't been fighting** yesterday.

F. Finish the sentences with the correct continuous form of the verbs.

1. I wish I (wait/not) _____ for so long yesterday.

2. She wishes she (relax) _____ right now.

3. He wishes he (work/not) _____ right now.

4. I wish it (rain/not) _____ when we got married.

5. I wish she (listen/not) _____ to my conversation with you yesterday.

6. I wish I (study/not) _____ . I want to go to the movie.

7. She wishes she (grow) _____ tomatoes in her garden this summer.

8. I wish you (sit) _____ when I told you the bad news.

9. I wish she (cook/not) _____ broccoli for dinner. I hate it!

10. He wishes he (drive/not) _____ when he was so tired.

11. I wish I (sit) _____ on the beach right now.

12. I wish it (snow) _____ so we could go skiing.

13. He wishes I (talk/not) _____ on the phone when he was trying to study.

12-1 FUTURE PERFECT

❶ The future perfect is used to talk about an activity in the future that will happen before another event in the future.

I will go to school at 9 A.M. Joseph will call me at 11 A.M. By the time Joseph calls me, I **will have gone** to school already.

❷ It is also used to talk about an activity in the future in relation to a specific time in the future.

By September 14th, my parents *will have returned* from their vacation in Hawaii.

❸ The future perfect uses the structure *will have* + the past participle of the main verb.

| At 2 A.M. | I
she | will have been | awake for 20 hours. |

A. Finish the sentences about <u>you</u> using the future perfect.

1. By the time I go to bed tonight, _____

2. At 12 P.M. tomorrow, _____

3. By the time I'm 50 years old, _____

4. By the time I get to school tomorrow, _____

5. By 2020, _____

6. By the time I have grandchildren, _____

7. By the time I finish school, _____

8. By this time next year, _____

9. By my next birthday, _____

10. By the time the weekend comes, _____

12-2 FUTURE PERFECT CONTINUOUS

❶ The future perfect continuous is used to talk about the duration of an activity in the future that will begin before another event in the future.

> Bill will move to New York in August. Andrea will move to New York in November. By the time Andrea moves to New York, Bill **will have been living** there for three months.

❷ It is also used to talk about the duration of an activity in the future in relation to a specific time in the future.

> By 3:00 P.M., **I will have been sitting** here for three hours.

❸ The future perfect continuous uses the structure *will have been* + verb + *–ing*.

| In August, | I / she | will have been working here | for 2 years. |

B. Read each scenario and then write a sentence using the future perfect continuous.

1. I will start studying French in September. You will start studying French the next January.

   By the time you start studying French, <u>*I will have been studying French for four months.*</u>

2. Jim will start working at our family's store in 2012. I will start working there in 2015.

   By the time I start working at our family's store, _____

3. Vinny will go to sleep at 8 P.M. tonight. His parents will go to bed at 11 P.M. tonight.

   By 11 P.M., _____

4. Albert will start doing his homework at 3 P.M. His father will get home at 5 P.M.

   _____

5. I will move to Seoul next year. My friend will move there a year after that.

   _____

6. Erin will arrive at the shopping mall at 12 P.M. I won't arrive there until 1 P.M. so she

   will have to wait for me. _____

❶ Some phrasal verbs have a literal meaning—the meaning of the combined words comes from the separate words.

stand up	throw away*
sit down	put up*

❷ The meaning of some other phrasal verbs is not literal, but still possible to guess from the separate words.

call off*	=	cancel
carry on	=	keep going
think over*	=	consider

❸ Some phrasal verbs are *idiomatic.* This means that the combination of words have a special meaning that is different from the meaning of the separate words.

give up	=	stop trying
pass away	=	die
put off*	=	wait, delay

*These phrasal verbs can take an object. A noun object can go after the phrasal verb or between the two parts of the phrasal verb. A pronoun object can only go between the two parts of the phrasal verb.

You should **call off** the meeting.
You should **call** the meeting **off**.
You should **call** it **off**

C. Write the correct phrasal verbs in the blanks. Be careful to write the phrasal verb in the correct verb tense.

call off	give up	put off	stand up
carry on	pass away	sit down	think over

1. The team didn't _____ even though they were losing by a lot.

2. After the game, the coach _____ talking to the team for a few minutes so that they could talk to the fans first.

3. I hope they won't _____ the game because of the rain.

4. Jacob played in the game today even though he was sad that his uncle _____ yesterday.

5. Everyone in the crowd _____ to see better when one of the players got hurt.

6. Bob says he needs to _____ whether he wants to be on the team again next year because he might not have the time.

7. The band _____ playing even though our team was losing.

8. The players _____ on the bench when they weren't playing.

Phrasal Verb + Preposition	Meaning
come up with	produce
cut down on	reduce the amount of
drop in on	casually visit
get along with	have a good relationship with
get back to	resume; return to
give in to	finally agree to

1 Some phrasal verbs can be followed by a preposition.

2 The object, noun or pronoun, always goes after the preposition.

I **dropped in on** Joe to see if he was feeling better.
I **dropped in on** him to see if he was feeling better.

D. Unscramble the sentences with phrasal verbs.

1. everybody / gets / she / Camille / with / along / meets /.

   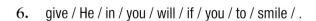

2. going / to / I'm / back / my homework / to / get /.

   _____

3. should / down / Austin / on / candy / cut / candy /.

   _____

4. call / They / if / off / it / it / might / snows / .

   _____

5. me / dropped / on / work / Kathleen / in / at / today /.

   _____

6. give / He / in / you / will / if / you / to / smile / .

   _____

7. with / came / believable / a / She / up / story /.

   _____

8. it / long / put / off / Don't / too / .

   _____

Credits